nF418657

ASK Ben ABOUT.....

AUTISM

<u>*A Message From Ben*</u>

"I hope this book helps people to understand how kids with autism feel and think, so that others can support them more, be more patient and help them find their abilities, what I call "superpowers" - Ben Blanchet

<u>*Dedication*</u>

This book is dedicated to my Pop Pop because he always supports everything I do.

<u>*Thank You*</u>

A special thank you to my cousin Chris Guercio, for his help with the cover of this book. Also, thank you to my followers for supporting me on my mission to teach people to see the abilities in kids who have autism.

Table of Contents

About Ben - by Angela Blanchet

Ask Ben Questions - by Ben Blanchet

Chapter 1
1. Did you ever line things up?
2. Do you listen to the same thing over and over again?
3. Do you think the weather affects your autism?
4. Did you ever try to elope or wander off?
5. Do you observe objects close to your eyes?

Chapter 2
1. How are you affected by different smells?
2. Do you have vocal stims?
3. Are you attracted to the water?
4. Do you ever laugh at inappropriate times?
5. Do you like to spin?

Chapter 3
1. Do you associate people only with certain places?
2. How do lights affect you?
3. Do you need to follow a routine?
4. How do different sounds make you feel?
5. What calms you down?

Chapter 4
1. Is pain a sensory overload?
2. Do you like to swing or rock?
3. Do you ask the same question over and over again?

4. Did you notice things around you even though you were nonverbal?
5. Is it hard for you to make eye contact?

Chapter 5
1. Can you hear things from far away?
2. Was it hard for you to eat different foods?
3. What would you like teachers or paraprofessionals to know about autism?
4. Is it hard for you to sleep?
5. Why do you flap your hands?

Chapter 6
1. Do you cover your ears?
2. Is it difficult for you to go to stores?
3. Do you have a hard time brushing your teeth?
4. It is challenging for you to talk on the telephone?
5. How does your therapy dog help you?

Chapter 7
1. Did you ever press your chin into your mom or dad?
2. Is there a special way you memorize things?
3. Is it hard for you to get a haircut?
4. How did you find out you have autism?
5. Do you tell people you have autism?
6. Do you think people treat you differently because you have autism?

<u>**About Ben**</u>

Ben is 14 years old and has autism. Ben was diagnosed with autism when he was just under two years old. He was non verbal for many years, with most of his speech being self-talk and echolalia from his favorite TV shows. By seven years old, Ben was putting a few words together unprompted, and by 11 years old, he had developed more natural, spontaneous speech. Throughout these years, Ben presented with the typical autism behaviors….self-talk and echolalia, stimulatory behaviors (stimming, flapping, rocking), vocal stims (humming, grunting), OCD (obsessive compulsive disorder) and major sensory meltdowns (from sounds, smells, bright lights). However, despite the autism challenges, Ben demonstrated some amazing abilities, what he refers to as his "superpowers". Ben has a perfect pitch, amazing memory, the ability to speed read, and he has a keen sense of direction. At 13 years old, after seeing a Marvel superhero movie, Ben wrote a book called "Maybe Autism Is My Superpower", followed by a sequel, "Maybe Autism Is YOUR

Superpower". These books were well received around the world and sparked a movement of children and families of autism sharing and focusing on autism abilities. Ben has met hundreds of families of autism at book signing events, as well as on his social media pages. Many parents of children who have autism have asked Ben direct questions about his autism, in hopes of gaining a better understanding of their own children who are younger, new to autism or developmentally behind Ben. Not until the past few years, however, has Ben been able to express the answers to these questions. This book is a compilation of answers Ben has provided about his autism over the past year. We hope that by sharing this, people will get a better glimpse into the "why" children with autism act, feel, or respond a certain way. Many of Ben's answers have even surprised me. I am so happy he is able to put words to these questions now, so that he can help others better understand, support and teach children with autism. - Ben's Mom (Angela Blanchet)

<u>**Chapter 1**</u>

1. Ask Ben: Did you ever line things up?

Yes! When I was younger I would line up a lot of my toys. I would love to line up animals, letters, numbers, vehicles and my Thomas trains. It would make me feel good because I couldn't talk and lining things up brought order to things for me. Putting things in order would always make me feel better. Sometimes, I would put things in number order, size order or color order. Now that I am older, and can talk a lot more, I only line things up in my *Minecraft* world that I build in the video game *Minecraft.* I line up different cities that I build. That still helps me to feel good!

2. Ask Ben: Do you listen to the same thing over and over again?

I often listen to the same part of a song, TV show or movie over and over again. I like to find the part of a song that has musical pitches that I like and has a good rhythm. It relaxes me to play this over and over again. With TV shows and movies, I look for the funny parts and play them over and over again because when I laugh, it makes me feel good too. Finding one piece of a song, show or movie is like a mental treatment that relaxes me. Some people like to meditate to make themselves feel better when they are stressed out. I think that for me, and a lot of kids with autism, listening to the same part of a TV show, movie, video or song is like meditation. It makes us feel good and also takes away the other noises that are around us, which can be stressful. It is something we do to feel better.

3. Ask Ben: Do you think the weather affects your autism?

Yes, I do think the weather affects my autism, and it is something that my mom noticed a long time ago, when I was younger. When the weather was cloudy, rainy or stormy, my autism behaviors would be more challenging. It would be harder for me to focus, I would have more stims like hand flapping and rocking. I would also have more headaches. When I would have a harder time with my autism, my mom would look at the barometer. A barometer measures the air pressure. If the barometer was rising, I would have an easier day. If the barometer was falling, I would have a harder day with more sensory issues. I would need more sensory input and my parents would give me things like squeeze balls, weighted blankets, lap pads, fidget toys and more tight hugs. My parents and Pop Pop made me a ball pit out of a large bin with ping pong balls in it and I would sit in there for a while too. This would help me a lot. I would like to swing more on days that the weather wasn't good. I had an indoor swing for this.

4. Ask Ben: Did you ever try to elope or wander off?

Yes. I would do this when I was younger and it would make my parents worried. I would wander to look at things that I was very interested in or ocd (obsessive compulsive) about, such as elevators, exit signs and automatic door signs. I have always loved elevators. My favorite brand is

Schindler because I love the chimes it makes in the key of B and G. If I was in an office building that had an elevator, I would try to run to check out what brand of elevator they had. I would also run to look at exit signs and to watch automatic doors open and close. This made my parents worried, so they got me a GPS tracker to track my location in case I wandered away and they couldn't find me.

One time, when I was about 6 years old, I tried to leave my house to walk to *Chuck E Cheese*. I knew exactly how to get there because I have a great memory for directions. My mom saw me walk out the door toward the street and she asked me where I was going. I didn't speak much back then, but I was able to say "Chuck E Cheese" and the names of the roads that I had memorized to get there. This made my parents very nervous, so they got me a therapy dog that my family taught to follow me around the house and alert them to where I was. I am now 14 years old. I don't elope or wander anymore, but sometimes I run off, if something really bothers my sensory system, like the sounds of some bugs, or certain loud music played by certain instruments in a certain pitch.

5. Ask Ben: Do you observe objects close to your eyes?

Yes! I would very often look at the things out of the corner of my eyes, when I was younger. I would take a pen or pencil, or a toy and slowly move it in front of my eyes from the side. It is called "side glancing". I would also like to close one eye and look at my toys. I did this because it would create a different picture of what I was seeing. Many therapists call this "visual stimming", but I call it "creating a different picture". It felt good to look at things differently. My brain really liked these pictures. My parents knew I liked to see things from different angles, and create different pictures with my eyes, so they bought me a lot of view masters and kaleidoscopes and I really enjoyed them.

Chapter 2

1. Ask Ben: How are you affected by different smells?

I am very affected by different smells. Some smells bother me and some calm me down. I am very bothered by the smell of strong cheeses and I don't like going into Italian restaurants because of the types of cheeses I smell there. But, some smells calm me down too. When I was little and I was really stressed, I would smell my mom's hair. That always made me feel better. When I do my school work, I like using smencils (scented pencils). It relaxes me while doing my school work. My favorite scents are chocolate and cherry. I also love to smell my dad's coffee. It makes me feel relaxed. I also like the smell of lavender. My mom puts this essential oil on my wrists and the back of my neck to help me feel calm and to sleep better. I think kids with autism have a sensitivity to smell and different smells may bother some kids that don't bother other kids.

2. Ask Ben: Do you have vocal stims?

Yes, I do. Vocal stims are sounds kids with autism make like humming or grunting. Many people think that kids who have autism and can talk don't make vocal sounds, but I think many of them do. Even at 14 years old, I still grunt and make humming noises. I do this mostly when I am excited or upset. I make sounds, instead of using words or talking. Instead of saying "I'm excited" or "I'm upset", I grunt or hum because it's easier and it feels good. It's just a different way to express my emotion. When my mom hears me making these noises, she will try to get me to talk to her instead. Sometimes she asks me, "What are you thinking about?"or "Why are you so excited?" or "Why are you upset?". If I am able to talk about it, then the vocal sounds I am making stop. I also make humming sounds sometimes, so that I don't hear other noises around me that may be bothering me.

3. Ask Ben: Are you attracted to the water?

When I was younger, water was good and bad for me. I didn't like getting even one drip of water on my clothes, so my mom would always bring a change of clothes for me, in case I got wet. For a few years, I would only wear rainboots on my feet when I went outside, in case there was a puddle or something wet on the ground. I don't need to do this anymore. If I get my clothes wet now, I'm not happy about it, but I don't freak out anymore. Water was also very calming for me. If something really upset me, my mom would put me in the bath. I loved the sound the water made when I splashed. I would also play with a water table, so I can hear the splashes. I used to not like swimming in a pool because it really bothered me to get my face wet, but as I got older, that also got easier. I love the pool now because you can hear a lot of splashing and also because I really like the way the light reflects off the water. I like to see the colors, it's calming to me. I think children with autism are drawn to water because of both the sound of the waves and the colors that you can see in the water.

4. Ask Ben: Do you ever laugh at inappropriate times?

I don't do this now, but, when I was younger, I used to laugh at inappropriate times very often. When I was a little kid, I would enjoy watching cartoons like *Bugs Bunny* and *The Road Runner*. In the cartoons, if someone got hurt, or ran over by a car and became flattened, I thought it was very funny! Even only a few years ago, I would laugh when people got hurt or when they were sad. My mom had to explain to me that the way cartoon characters feel is very different then the way people feel in real life. That took me a long time to understand. Now, I am able to understand and I only laugh to myself when I think about funny things. I like to make up TV shows and cartoons in my mind that are funny. It makes me feel good to think about the characters and how they can do funny things.

5. Ask Ben: Do you like to spin?

When I was younger, I would like to spin a lot! There were a few different ways I would spin.

Sometimes, I would twist my swing and then let go so I would spin around really fast. Sometimes, I would just stand in the middle of the floor and spin in circles. Sometimes, I would spin on a dizzy disc, which is like a sit and spin without the middle piece. I would be able to spin really fast on it. It would take me a really long time to get dizzy. My neurologist told my parents that this is because my nervous system was still developing and that for kids with autism, the vestibular system (which is the part of the nervous system in the ear that controls balance) takes a longer time to mature. So, I was wanting to spin a lot, to help develop my nervous system. This is why my parents always let me spin, but of course made sure I spun around in a safe place. I know that most kids with autism crave the feeling of spinning. As I got older, I didn't need to spin as much anymore.

Chapter 3

1. Ask Ben: Do you associate people only with certain places?

Yes, I do and it has been really challenging for me over the years. When I associate someone from one place it is very hard for me to see them in a different place. I take music production classes and one time I saw the owner of the company at a grocery store near me. It felt really weird to see him somewhere else. I didn't even want to say hello. Also, I used to take drum lessons with a man named Justin and piano lessons with a man named Steve back to back at a music school. Lessons with Steve came first, and the lesson with Justin was after. If I would see Justin before I saw Steve, in the waiting room of the music school, I would hide and close my eyes. It was very uncomfortable for me because it wasn't time to see Justin yet. I was seeing him at the wrong time. My mom would have to help me open my eyes and say hello. Also, my parents wanted to take me to Justin's house to see how he set up his home studio. I didn't want to go because I only associated him with the music school. My mom would tell me to try one time and if it felt too weird, I wouldn't have to try again. Sometimes, when I try one time to see someone at a different place, I make a new association and it helps me. I am now able to take lessons also at Justin's home music studio, even though it was hard for me at first. I can't really explain why it's like this, but I think this a challenge for many other kids with autism.

2. Ask Ben: How do lights affect you?

Sometimes lights stress me out and sometimes they relax me. When I was little, I would cry a lot when I was in a store, bank or post office that had fluorescent lighting. This type of lighting really bothered me and gave me a headache. No one really knew why I was crying, until I was older and could explain it more. My parents would constantly have to take me out of stores, banks, post offices and some restaurants, to calm me down. Also, when I was younger, sunlight going into my eyes would cause me to have a type of seizure called petit mal or absence seizure. This doesn't happen from the sunlight anymore. Also, there is a light that shines from my neighbor's house and reflects in the trees. I call it "reflection" and I have a really hard time looking out the window at night, if the reflection is there. It bothers me so much that my parents even moved my bedroom to a different room, so that I can't see the reflection light out the window anymore. Lights on flashlights and Iphones also bother me. I wear bluelight glasses when I use my phone, computer or tablet and they help me a lot. There are some lights that relax me and calm me down. I love looking at city lights and lights on cars on the parkways. I also love Christmas lights. I really like it when there are a lot of lights together. It's soothing.

3. Ask Ben: Do you need to follow a routine?

When I was younger, I followed a very strict routine. I still like a routine, but I am much more flexible now. When my routine changed, I would get very nervous and cry a lot and my parents would always tell me it is important to be FLEXIBLE. They would say that word a lot to me and, as I got older, I learned it is ok to be flexible. I am a homeschooler and on school days, I liked to see my routine and schedule on a whiteboard. I would erase the work I completed and see what was left to do. I liked to cross things off or erase them on the board. I also had very strict bedtime and eating routines, but that was really because I have OCD (obsessive compulsive disorder) and I set those routines for myself. I would go to bed at the same time every night. I wanted to take a bath every night at 8:00 pm and get out of the bathtub at 8:30 pm and brush my teeth at exact times too. I would wake up every morning at 7:00 am. I would do this even if I wasn't feeling well. My mom would tell me to rest and sleep longer some days, but I couldn't because it was a routine and it really upset me if I broke the routine. I would feel anxious and nervous. I also wanted to eat lunch at exactly 12:00 pm. In my town, we have a 12:00 pm alarm that rings from our firehouse, so I knew when it was exactly 12:00 pm. I would sit at the kitchen table with my lunch and wait until I heard the fire alarm ring and then I would start to eat. I would always eat the large half first. I would measure the two halves of the sandwich against each other. I also did this with french fries. I would measure them and eat the smallest ones first. At dinner, if I had chicken nuggets and french fries, I would always eat the chicken first and then the potatoes. I would always eat the meat or entree before I ate a side dish. My meal routines and OCD are much better now. I learned to be more flexible as I became older. My parents still tell me that it is great to be flexible. Another routine I have is always wanting to take the decorations from the holidays down as soon as the holiday is over. I want the next decorations for the next holiday up right away. It still bothers me to wait to decorate for the next holiday, but I am more flexible about it now.

4. Ask Ben: How do different sounds make you feel?

There are sounds that bother me and sounds that make me feel good. The sounds that bothered me when I was younger are different than the sounds that bother me today. When I was younger, the sound of the vacuum cleaner was horrible to my ears. My mom couldn't vacuum at all if I was in the house. My dad would have to take me for a ride in the car, so my mom could vacuum. Also, the sound of a pan sizzling on the stove with oil in it was very hard for me to listen to. My parents had to tell me if they were going to cook with a pan on the stove, so I could hide in my room. The sound of our dishwasher also bothered me a lot. I'm not really sure why this noise bothered me. I just know that it did. My parents would run the dishwasher when I was sleeping at night. The good thing is that none of these sounds bother me anymore. I also hated the sounds of fire alarms and emergency alerts. These sounds still bother me sometimes. As I got older, some new sounds began to bother me, such as bugs buzzing, violins, flutes and opera music. These sounds still bother me today. I wear headphones when I know I will be outside or around music with violins or flutes. Loud DJ music used to bother me a lot too. I couldn't go to parties or weddings. Now that I play a lot of music instruments myself, including drums, it doesn't bother me too much anymore. One thing that helped me a lot with the sounds that bothered me was someone giving me a warning that the sound was coming (if they could), so I could get my headphones or go into a different room. It also helped me a lot to listen to sounds that were soothing, after listening to a sound that bothered me. Some of my favorite sounds include ride cymbals, electric piano tones, and certain chimes.

Some of my favorite electric piano tones are Yamaha's iconic DX7 voice and the rhodes voice. When I was in Tampa International Airport, I noticed the pre-announcement chime on the overhead speakers, and I really liked it. It was in the key of B. I have perfect pitch and can hear what key different sounds make. Other chimes I love to listen to are elevator chimes. My favorite is the Schindler elevator chime because it makes the B and G notes. Sometimes, to make myself feel good and relax, I listen to these chimes on YouTube. I also enjoy listening to the theme songs of certain TV shows including *Everybody Loves Raymond, The George Lopez Show*, *The King of Queens* and *Friends.* I also love listening to the *Warner Brothers* logo tune from 2003. I listen to it on YouTube also and it is very calming. I think that some sounds feel good and some sounds bother kids who have autism, and I think it is different for each kid. I also think the sounds that bother kids who have autism change as they get older. I always carry my headphones with me, just in case.

5. Ask Ben: What calms you down?

When I need to calm down, it is usually because of a sensory or OCD issue I am having. What calmed me down when I was younger is different than what calms me down today. When I was younger, swinging was my favorite way to calm down. I had an outdoor and indoor swing, so I was always able to swing, even when the weather was bad. Spinning on a dizzy disc helped me a lot too. My parents would give me sensory toys to play with like squeeze balls and they would put weighted blankets on me too or sit me in a bin filled with ping pong balls. I even had a machine called a squeeze machine (steam roller) that I would crawl through and it would give me the feeling of having a tight hug. Chewing gum also helped me to relax. When I was really upset, if those things didn't work, my parents would give me a bath, or drive me in the car. Both the water and riding in a car are very soothing to me. I like riding in the car because I love the sound of the motor. Watching my favorite TV shows and cartoons also helped me to calm down. Now that I am older, I don't have a swing, but I do like to rock in a rocking chair. Also, playing musical instruments (piano, drums or ukulele) and listening to music relaxes me. Watching comedy tv shows is also another way I calm down. Funny things make me laugh and feel better. Talking to myself also calms me down a lot. I did that a lot more when I was younger. I still do that today because it makes me feel good, but I try to just do that at home.

Chapter 4

1.Ask Ben: Is Pain A Sensory Overload?

Pain can cause me to have a sensory overload. It depends on what is hurting and what my sensory issues are. If I have a headache and hear sounds that bother my ears at the same time, that can be a sensory overload for me. So, if I am in pain, I have to be careful not to be around other things that bother my senses. If I have a skin rash that is bothering me, then it can become a sensory overload if I have to wear clothes that bother me at the same time. When I was younger, I would only wear tank tops, because the feeling of clothes on my arms bothered me. When pain is at the same time as sensory issues, it is a lot harder to have the pain.

2. Ask Ben: Do you like to swing or rock?

Yes I do! I loved going on the swing when I was younger and could swing for hours. I would like to swing when my school work was done or when I was stressed out from sensory stuff. It would calm me down and make me feel better. I liked when my speech therapists would talk to me when I was on the swing. Swinging would help me to talk back to them. I still enjoy swinging, but now that I am older, I use a rocking chair more than a swing. I take rocking chair breaks when I am doing my school work. Rocking is also very soothing. This is why kids who have autism rock even when they don't have a rocking chair to sit on. They are soothing themselves.

3. Ask Ben: Do you ask the same question over and over again?

I know a lot of kids who have autism, like me, feel better when they can hear the answer to a question over and over again. It is like an ocd. I'm not really sure why it calmed me down, I just know that it did. One question that I liked to ask my parents over and over again was, "When are we getting more food"? I would ask this question because it would bother me a lot if food was running low in the house. I would never want to eat the last piece of bread or last cookie or drink the last of the juice. It would make me feel better to see a lot of the same food. My parents would tell me when they were going to buy more food, but I wanted to keep asking them, so I could hear the answer over and over again, to make sure it is the same answer. I would also ask my parents over and over again, "What time are you going to bed tonight"? I asked this question a lot because it would bother me when they went to bed after midnight because that was the next day. So, I would ask the question over and over again to make sure they were going to bed before midnight. To help me not have to ask the same questions a lot, my mom would write the answer to the questions in a book. If I wanted to ask the question again, she would tell me to go read the book because the answer is the same. That would help me to not have to ask the same questions as often.

4. Ask Ben: Did you notice things around you even though you were nonverbal?

Yes! When I was younger, even though I didn't speak, I would notice things around me. Some of the things I would notice were *Exit* signs, *Do Not Enter* signs and *Automatic Caution Door* signs. I would notice elevator brands and the pitches they make. I would be able to remember where I saw the same brand of elevators. I would also notice the brands of cash register machines and the pitches they make. I would notice *CoinStar* machines and reverse vending machines too. Also, when my parents drove me around in the car, I would notice all of the grocery stores and the water towers. I would memorize them and then I would know what town I was in based on the grocery stores or water towers I would see. When I got older, I started to also notice real estate signs outside of buildings and posters, signs and directories inside of buildings. I would also memorize these. My ears are able to notice music playing overhead in a store, alerts on people's iPhones and pre- announcement chimes in places like airports. I notice them and the pitch they are in. Even when a kid who has autism is not speaking much, this doesn't mean they aren't noticing things and memorizing things that are around them. Usually, the things we notice are very different from the things our family or friends are noticing.

5. Ask Ben: Is it hard for you to make eye contact?

Making eye contact with people was a lot harder for me when I was younger, than it is for me now. It was hard for me to use two of my senses (hearing and seeing) at the same time. When people spoke to me, they liked me to look at them also, but I was using my ears to listen to them. I needed to separate the listening and the looking. So, just because I wasn't making eye contact, didn't mean I wasn't listening to them or understanding them. I think many kids who have autism have a hard time with making eye contact.

It can be uncomfortable and overwhelming to our senses. But, as I got older, it got easier for me. One thing my parents did was wear funny eye glasses when they spoke to me, so that I would look at them and not feel as stressed out because it was funny. They wore red glasses and it made me want to look at them. I think that helped me alot!

Chapter 5

1.Ask Ben: Can you hear things from far away?

Yes! I can hear things from very far away and I have met other kids who have autism who can hear things that are really far away too. My mom and dad call my ears supersonic. I can hear train whistles, fire alarms, bugs buzzing, music playing and the ice cream truck before many other people hear it. Sometimes, when a noise is bothering me, my parents don't understand why because they don't hear it as loudly as I do. They have to ask me what I am hearing. This is why I always have my headphones with me.

2.Ask Ben: Was it hard for you to eat different foods?

Yes. It was very hard for me to eat different foods when I was younger. For many years, I would only eat chicken nuggets, corn dogs, mini donuts, yogurt and snap peas. The foods I would eat changed a little bit each year. There were foods that were very hard for me to touch and foods that were very hard for me to smell. The texture and smell had to be just right to eat it. I also preferred to eat finger foods because I didn't like the feel of a fork in my mouth. My parents would make me protein or health shakes to sip on,to make sure I was getting all of the nutrition that I needed. I know that this is a challenge for most kids with autism. I can't really explain why it got easier for me to try different foods. I think I just grew out of some of the food sensory challenges as I got older. There are still foods that I don't like to smell, like strong cheeses (parmesan and pecorino romano), soy sauce and peppers. I have challenges with many vegetables including mushrooms. I have a hard time going into Italian restaurants because of the smell, but I do eat many more foods now.

3. Ask Ben: What would you like teachers or paraprofessionals to know about autism?

I have been a homeschooled student since kindergarten, but if I were to go to school, I would want teachers, therapists and paraprofessionals to know a few things about autism. One is that kids with autism need to take frequent breaks to help calm down their sensory system. If teachers could give sensory breaks that would help a lot. Also, kids with autism like to be warned if loud noises are coming. So, if there is going to be a fire drill, it would really help to be warned about it, so we know when to cover our ears or use headphones. For me, rainy days have been harder to learn because I would have headaches and more sensory and ocd challenges. I love to put my feet on a stretchy band on a chair or desk in front of me. It helps me stay in my seat. Highlighters have helped me to read because I don't lose my place if I look away. Also, it really helps to know what is coming next and not be surprised. I always liked to see a schedule on a board, so I could cross things out or erase them when I was finished and could see what comes next.

4. Ask Ben: Is it hard for you to sleep?

Falling asleep is often a challenge for me, ever since I was little. My neurologist told my parents to give me melatonin because a lot of kids with autism don't make enough melatonin, but it doesn't always help me. It used to help me more when I was younger. My mom puts calming essential oils on me at night. I really love the smell, so that helps me a little too, but trying to fall asleep really stresses me out. Going for a long walk and taking a bath before bed sometimes help relax me and make it easier to fall asleep. I think a lot of kids who have autism struggle with sleep. I'm not really sure why. The nights that I don't sleep much cause me to have more sensory issues the next day, so I will need more help to relax my sensory system the next day.

5. Ask Ben: Why do you flap your hands?

I flap my hands a lot, especially when I am excited, or upset, or when I am trying to talk. A lot of times, it is hard for me to use words to explain that I am really excited or upset, so I flap my hands instead. I think many other kids who have autism also flap their hands. This kind of movement helps us feel better. Sometimes, I flap my hands a lot more when I am trying to speak. It helps me come out with the words to say. My doctor explained to my mom that flapping my hands helps my neural pathways for speech. So, my parents don't ask me to stop flapping my hands because they know it is helping me to feel better and talk more.

Chapter 6

1. Ask Ben: Do you cover your ears?

I do cover my ears from sensitive things. I have perfect pitch and I know the notes or pitch of many things that I hear, even things in my house like microwaves, tea kettles, doorbells and spoons and forks hitting the bowls and plates. I think there are a lot of kids with autism who have perfect pitch and that's great for playing music, but it also can make it challenging because our ears are very sensitive to pitches. When I was younger, I was more bothered by pitches than I am today. The sound of many of the different songs on the radio and appliances in my house bothered me a lot. When kids with autism cover their ears, it could be because they have perfect pitch, like me. I think we cover our ears because our ears are special.

2. *Ask Ben: Is it difficult for you to go to stores?*

I like going to stores now, because I like to look at the brands of scanners and check out machines in the grocery stores. My favorite scanner is the NCR because it scans in the F note. When I was younger, it was a lot harder for me to go to stores. I didn't want to go into any store, if I didn't like the scanner they had. Also, there were many different sensory things in stores that would bother me. The lights would bother my head because they are really bright. The freezers or refrigerators would sometimes make a humming sound. The smells of different foods would bother me, especially cheeses. I would be very nervous about hearing a fly in the store, because often flies get into grocery stores and the sound of the buzzing would bother my ears a lot. It would also make me anxious to see some food running low in stock because I didn't like when food would run out. I don't have as many issues with grocery stores anymore, but I do bring my headphones with me still, in case I hear a fly buzzing or music that doesn't sound good to my ears.

3. Ask Ben: Do you have a hard time brushing your teeth?

I had a very hard time brushing my teeth when I was younger, especially when my teeth were loose because I didn't want them to fall out. Losing my teeth was a bad ocd I had. I didn't like when things couldn't come back again and everytime I lost a tooth, I wanted it back in my mouth again. It made me very anxious. I also didn't like the sensory feeling of a toothbrush or toothpaste in my mouth. I would only use the fruit flavored toothpastes. As I became older, and my adult teeth all came in, brushing my teeth became easier. I really like vibrating toothbrushes the best because they feel better in my mouth and I now prefer to use the mint toothpaste.

4. Ask Ben: Is it challenging for you to talk on the telephone?

Telephone conversations are challenging for me because I can't see the person I am talking to and because I don't always know when to end the conversation. When I was younger and people would talk to me on the phone, I would hand the phone to my mom and she would tell me that the people were still talking to me and the conversation wasn't over. So, when I was able to speak, she taught me some sentences to say to let people know that I was done talking to them, and I still use these sentences today. I will say, "It was nice talking to you, good-bye" or "I have to go now". That was difficult for me to learn, so my parents would set up practice phone calls for me. I would practice having phone conversations with my grandparents, aunts, uncles and cousins. My mom also taught me to listen, answer and ask. I needed to learn to listen to what the person is saying, answer their question and then ask a question. This is still something I practice because it's not easy for me.

5. Ask Ben: How does your therapy dog help you?

My parents got me a therapy dog, named Lucca, when I was 7 years old. He is a chocolate lab. My parents were worried about me because I would sometimes try to walk out of the house, and when they called out to me, I wouldn't answer them because I wasn't using my words back then. A trainer came to our house and taught Lucca how to find me. We would play hide and go seek with Lucca. I would hide and my parents would tell Lucca to "find Ben" and then they would take him to me. After a few weeks, Lucca learned to find me on his own. Lucca was taught to follow me around the house and alert my parents if I left the house or got close to the door. I mostly liked that Lucca would sit with me during my therapy sessions at home. He would sit under the table and I could press my feet into him. That would feel good and calm me down. Lucca still sits under my feet when I sit at the table. He would also sit in the bathroom when I took a bath and he would go outside with me when I was on the swing. I think therapy dogs are great for kids with autism and can help them in a lot of different ways.

Chapter 7

1. Ask Ben: Did you ever press your chin into your mom or dad?

Pressing my chin into my mom is something I did very often when I was younger and still do today. Also, when I was younger and my grandma would come over and watch TV with me, she would sit on the couch and I would stand behind her and press my chin into her head. Recently, when I was at a crowded store, I became anxious because people were coughing and sneezing and I am afraid to get sick because I have an immune deficiency. I went over to my mom for a tight hug and then pressed my chin into her. This helped me feel much better! Sometimes, when I am sitting at a table or my desk to do school work, I put my hand under my chin and press it in to relax myself. "Chin digs" are something kids with autism do to calm down. I don't know how to explain it. The only thing I can explain is that it helps me to relax, just like pressing my feet into something helps me relax too. It's comforting.

2. Ask Ben: Is there a special way you memorize things?

Having a great memory is one of my autism superpowers. Many kids who have autism have super memories. Since I am a little kid, I use my index finger to help me memorize things. When I am memorizing math facts, I move my finger back and forth in the air and when I am memorizing piano music, I move my finger side to side along the keyboard. This helps me focus and memorize. It is something I have been doing since I am a little kid. It is like my brain is scanning things as my finger moves. I met other kids with autism who use their heads and move them up and down or side to side to help their brains scan what they are looking at. I am not sure why, but I think movement helps us memorize things.

3. *Ask Ben: Is it hard for you to get a haircut?*

It is still hard for me to get a haircut, but not as
hard as it used to be. Kids with autism have very
sensitive heads. Getting a haircut would hurt my
head. The buzzer would feel very uncomfortable to
me and the sound and feeling of the scissors
scared me a lot. There were a lot of other things in
the barber shop that bothered me too. The lights,
the sounds of the buzzers and hair dryers, getting
my head wet and the cape on my neck, and the
hair falling down and touching my skin were all
very hard for me. I was also very scared of getting
hair in my mouth. My mom would buzz my hair at
home because going into a barbershop was a
sensory overload. She would put weighted
blankets on my lap, give me sensory toys to hold
onto and squeeze and she would use a quiet
buzzer. I would need to take a lot of breaks. Now
that I am older and my head isn't as sensitive as it
used to be, it is easier for me. I can go to a
barbershop now. I still don't love the feeling of a
haircut and I want it to be done quickly, but it is
easier.

4. Ask Ben: How did you find out you have autism?

I can't remember not knowing that I have autism. When things were really hard for me, my parents would say "It's ok Ben, this is because your brain works differently because you have autism, but that also makes you special." So, I still think of autism as having a special brain. When my parents saw me use my "superpowers" (I have perfect pitch, a great memory, great sense of direction and can speed read), they would tell me that this was also because of my autism and having a special brain. I like knowing that I have autism and why some things are hard for me, but other things are easy for me.

5. Ask Ben: Do you tell people you have autism?

My parents often tell people I have autism, and so do I. I tell my new teachers when I take a class online because I think it helps them be more patient with me, especially if I have a hard time with attention and focus in the class. When I was little, my mom would pass out cards to people in the stores that seemed annoyed if I was having a sensory meltdown. The cards said, "My son has autism. He is not misbehaving. He is having a problem with the sensory environment. For more information about autism visit...." I hope it helped people understand more. I think sometimes because there is no look to autism, that people don't realize I have autism. They think autism should look a certain way. But, autism is on the inside not the outside. So, many people don't know I have autism because I look like every other kid, and they are surprised by some of my challenges. They are also surprised by some of my abilities and interests. This is why I like to tell people that I have autism.

6. Ask Ben: Do you think people treat you differently because you have autism?

I think some people are more kind and patient with me because I have autism. My family, teachers and therapists are very nice and patient with me, but I also think some people are not as patient with kids who have autism and could do better. I made my own list of the *"Top 10 Things People Can Say Differently To Kids Who Have Autism"*. *I posted this list on social media to help people understand more about what they could do or say better to help kids who have autism.*

1) *A lot of times people look at me and say, "You don't look like you have autism". They don't know that autism is not on the outside, but on the inside. When someone finds out I have autism, they shouldn't say "You don't look like you have autism" because that doesn't make sense.*

2) *When I was younger and I had some sensory meltdowns in the stores, some people would make comments. People have asked me, "Do you always behave like this"? They have also asked my mom, "What is wrong with him"? Instead of saying this, it would be nicer if someone asked, "Are you ok?" or "Is there something I can do to help you"?*

3) *Kids with autism often grunt or make humming sounds. People in public have told me to "shut up". I think this is very rude because we often can't help making these noises. Instead of being rude, I think it would be nicer if someone said, "Can you please be quiet" or "Can you lower your voice".*

4) *Kids who have autism have a hard time wearing a lot of different clothes because of sensory issues. When I was younger, I would only wear white tank tops with shorts or sweatpants and blue crocs. Sometimes people would ask me, "Didn't you wear that yesterday"? This wouldn't really*

upset me, but it would upset my mom because she always cleaned my clothes and she knew that I just couldn't wear anything else. Instead of asking this question, it would be nicer to say, "That must be your favorite shirt" or "That looks like your favorite outfit".

5) Kids with autism often move around a lot. The movement helps us calm down and feel better. We rock and flap our hands. Sometimes people say to me "Can you stop moving around so much?" This is not an easy thing for me to do, especially if there is a noise or smell that is bothering me. Sometimes, we just need the time and space to move. It's helpful if people could understand this.

6) Kids with autism have a very hard time with eye contact. A lot of people say "Look at me when I am talking to you". More people need to know that this is very hard and overwhelming for our senses. Also they need to know that just because we aren't looking at them, doesn't mean we aren't listening or understanding them.

7) Kids with autism have a really hard time trying different foods. Sometimes people would say to me "Just take a bite", to try to get me to eat different foods. It took me many years before I could just take a bite, but I eventually did and I eat a lot of different foods now. Saying, "Just take a bite", doesn't make it easier for us to take a bite. It doesn't change our sensory system.

8) When there are sounds that bother me, if I don't have my headphones, I will cover my ears. Some people think this is rude and will say, "Stop covering your ears". They think this means I don't want to listen to them. But what it really means is that there are other noises around that really hurt my ears. It would be nicer if people could ask, "What noise is bothering you?" and try to help fix the noise if they can.

9) *Kids with autism often talk to themselves out loud. This is another way we feel good and calm down. Some people have said to me, "Stop talking to yourself". This was not always easy for me to do, especially when I was younger and still learning how to use my words better. It would be nicer if people would talk to me about what I am talking to myself about. That would calm me down even more.*
10) *Kids with autism have a hard time waiting in line. I can't really explain why. I had a very hard time with this when I was younger. It was like an ocd. Plus, it is very hard to stay still for a long time. It would be nicer if someone would hold my place in line so I could get off the line and get the movement that I need to stay calm.*

conclusion

I hope this book helped you understand more about the "why" kids with autism seem different and why we have certain challenges so that you can teach, help and support us better. But remember, just because we have challenges and sensory difficulties, doesn't mean we don't have great abilities, what I call "superpowers".